What *do* we know about dinosaurs?

In our museums there are thousands of dinosaur bones, some made up into complete skeletons which tell us how big the animal was. But still we cannot really imagine what the dinosaurs looked like, or how they moved, can we?

This book contains many attractive, informative pictures to help us understand more about the dinosaurs who ruled the earth for millions of years. There is a dinosaur dictionary, which helps us with those hard-to-remember names, and question and answer sections to test our knowledge of the creatures which lived on the earth before humans ever existed.

# Contents

Published in Great Britain by
World International Publishing Limited.
P.O. Box 111, Great Ducie Street, Manchester M60 3BL.
Printed in Italy.
SBN 7235 7020 5.
Reprinted 1984.
2nd Reprint 1985.

# Let me tell you about...
# DINOSAURS

# What do we Know about Dinosaurs?

64 million years have passed since the last dinosaur roamed the earth, and as recently as 150 years ago man had still to discover the first evidence of their existence.

Yet these creatures from the far distant past have a special fascination for most of us, and somehow they seem almost as real as if they were living among us today.

Dinosaurs existed for some 140 million years, divided into three periods: the Triassic, the Jurassic and the Cretaceous. During that time their world changed radically, and they made many adaptations to the prevailing conditions of their particular times.

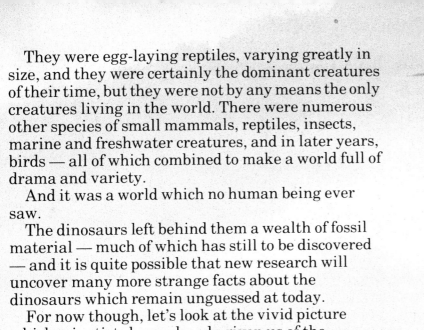

They were egg-laying reptiles, varying greatly in size, and they were certainly the dominant creatures of their time, but they were not by any means the only creatures living in the world. There were numerous other species of small mammals, reptiles, insects, marine and freshwater creatures, and in later years, birds — all of which combined to make a world full of drama and variety.

And it was a world which no human being ever saw.

The dinosaurs left behind them a wealth of fossil material — much of which has still to be discovered — and it is quite possible that new research will uncover many more strange facts about the dinosaurs which remain unguessed at today.

For now though, let's look at the vivid picture which scientists have already given us of the remarkable, long-vanished world of the creatures we know as dinosaurs.

# What was the World

The world in which the dinosaurs lived changed a great deal during the 140 million years of their existence.

## THE TRIASSIC PERIOD

### 225 - 190 million years ago

In the Triassic period the world was a very different place from the way we know it today.

The biggest difference was that all the continents as we know them were joined together in one great continent called Pangea. In the east, the Ocean of Tathys divided Pangea into two major land masses. The northern land mass, Laurasia, combined what we now know as North America, Europe and Asia, while the southern land mass, called Gondwanaland, included South America, Africa, India, Antarctica and Australia.

This explains why fossil remains are found all over the world, even though the countries they are found in may now be separated by oceans.

The climate was semi-tropical almost everywhere, and much of the land was desert, just as we know it, with sand dunes and life-giving oases. There were few plants at that time, but there is evidence of some ferns, mosses, bamboo-like plants called *Pelourdea*, conifers, and the monkey puzzle trees which are an ornamental favourite in today's gardens.

## THE JURASSIC PERIOD

### 190 - 136 million years ago

The great continent of Pangea began to split up during the Jurassic period, and different groups of animals began to evolve on each of the new land masses.

# of the Dinosaurs Like?

The climate became wetter, and there was more plant life, though still not in the great variety we know today. The conifers were still successful, and there were many palm-like trees called cycads. Some areas had dense, jungle-like undergrowth, composed mainly of different types of fern.

## THE CRETACEOUS PERIOD

### 136 - 64 million years ago

During the many million years of the Cretaceous period, the world began to become much more as we know it today. The land masses finally settled into the continents as we know them, though many features such as present-day mountain chains still did not exist, and for the most part the land was flat, with many warm seas and lagoons.

There was a tremendous variety of new plant life. Trees such as oak, magnolia and the giant redwood appeared in the early centuries, and later on much more woodland became established, with many of today's common trees, as well as figs and palms in the tropical lands.

## The Dinosaur Story Begins

Piecing together the complete story of the evolution of the dinosaurs is a complex business, even for the experts, and there is still much to be discovered and discussed today. The story begins in the Triassic period.

Let's take a look at some of the fascinating creatures which are known to have played an important part in the dinosaurs' development.

# THE PARAMAMMALS

The paramammals had some of the features of mammals and some of reptiles, and when the Triassic period began they had already been widespread and successful for many millions of years.

By the end of the period, though, their reptilian reign was over, and the only ones which remained had adapted to become true mammals. By then, as far as reptiles were concerned, the dinosaurs had become dominant.

# PROTEROSUCHUS

The crocodile-like *Proterosuchus* was a direct ancestor of the dinosaurs and, not surprisingly, of the crocodiles which we know today.

It was not very big, at around 1.5 metres long, but it was a powerful creature, with strong jaws and a good supply of sharp, tearing teeth. It would have eaten fish and some of the paramammals, and no doubt it would sometimes attack the lumbering plant-eater *Lystrosaurus*.

# LYSTROSAURUS

One of the oddest-looking of the paramammals was *Lystrosaurus*. This heavily-built creature was something like a hippopotamus, and it lived a similar sort of life, foraging in swamps and rivers for its diet of plants.

# ORNITHOSUCHUS

Possibly the first true dinosaur was a reptile named *Ornithosuchus*, which came later in the Triassic period.

It was about twice the size of *Proterosuchus*, and though still crocodilian in appearance it walked only on its hind legs, balancing its weight with its tail.

A fierce flesh-eater, it would have had few enemies, though later on in the period there might have been some danger from the other dinosaurs which had by then appeared.

In any case, would-be predators might well have thought twice about attacking *Ornithosuchus*, protected as it was by the bony plates on its back, and the sharp spines on its neck.

# COLEOPHYSIS

The age of the dinosaurs could probably be said to have begun with the arrival of *Ornithosuchus*, but at about the same time another creature appeared whose descendants were to form another branch of the dinosaur family.

This was another flesh-eater, known as *Coleophysis*, and though it did not look as fierce as *Ornithosuchus* it developed some very successful tactics in catching its prey.

It was lightly-built, with a long neck and tail, and it was extremely fast and agile. Whilst *Ornithosuchus* relied on brute force in attack, *Coleophysis* could keep pace with its prey, dart out its neck to bite, and grab at its food with the long fingers of its hands.

Both these flesh-eaters would probably have preyed on lizards, large insects, and later, the young of other dinosaurs.

# THECODONTSAURUS

*Thecodontsaurus* is interesting because it was probably the first dinosaur to try a plant-eating diet. At first it ate a mainly meat diet, supplemented with a little green food now and then, but eventually it changed completely to the vegetarian way of life.

This idea was soon to catch on amongst its relatives.

# PLATEOSAURUS

Another 'first' in the dinosaur world was achieved by the 6 metre long *Plateosaurus*, which was also another of the first plant-eaters.

Whether for social or for purely practical reasons of safety, *Plateosaurus* was probably the first of the dinosaurs to herd. We know this because of groups of footprint tracks which have been found, clearly showing several animals walking together.

Dinosaurs grew bigger because any large animal takes a long time to heat up or cool down. Therefore, their size helped them to keep their body temperature more stable.

# MELANOSAURUS

One of the first dinosaur giants, *Melanosaurus* was as long as seven men laid end to end.

# FABROSAURUS

All dinosaurs are classified into two groups, depending on the arrangement of their hip bones. Those with 'lizard-hips' are called *saurischians*, and those with 'bird-hips' are called *ornithischians*.

The small, 1 metre long, fast-running *Fabrosaurus* was the first of the *ornithischians*.

Some reference books describe a creature called *Heterodontsaurus* as the first true dinosaur, because of the shape of its jaws and teeth. No complete skeleton of *Heterodontsaurus* has ever been found.

# RHYNCHOSAURUS

*Rhynchosaurus* was a very strange-looking creature. It lived on the shores of lakes, and had strong, flat plates inside its jaws, which it used for breaking open hard seed pods, and cracking the shells of freshwater shellfish.

# TANYSTROPHEUS

This remarkable-looking lizard had a 3 metre long neck, which it probably used for fishing in shallow sea water, and maybe for reaching into rocky crevices. Oddly, although it was very long, the neck was not very flexible, so it is possible that it had some completely different purpose, which we do not yet understand.

At about this time, a reptile called *Proganochelys* made its first appearance. It was the first tortoise, and it was not much different from the animal we know today.

# The Triassic Seas...

The warm, shallow seas of the Triassic period teemed with life.
Undisputed masters of their kingdom were big, lizard-like reptiles which moved easily through the water searching for food.

# PLACODONTS

*Placodonts* were heavier creatures than the *nothosaurs*, and not so agile in the water. Their armoured backs were very tough, and when they were moving around on the sea bed, eating their prey of shellfish, they would present an impenetrable appearance to any creature which might have considered an attack.

Their teeth were adapted to their diet of shellfish. Peg-like front teeth would grasp the shells, and flat back teeth would grind them up, exposing the morsel of food inside. They would have had to have eaten a great many shellfish each day to keep their large, stocky bodies well nourished.

# NOTHOSAURS

The *nothosaurs* were the most abundant of these marine reptiles. They were large creatures, measuring anything up to 6 metres long, and their streamlined shape and long, flattened tails made them excellent swimmers.

They had webbed feet which they used as paddles, and they snapped at their prey with lethal mouths, full of sharp, pointed teeth.

The marine reptiles and the flying reptiles were not dinosaurs as such, but were important in the overall picture of reptile evolution.

# . . . and the Triassic Skies

There were numerous 'flying' creatures in the Triassic skies - but none of them were birds. The first bird *Archaeopteryx*, had yet to appear on the surface of the earth.

Most of these Triassic 'fliers' were not capable of true, flapping flight, but glided through the trees and parachuted down, rather like the flying squirrels of today.

# KUEHNEOSAURUS

This lizard was probably one of the first airborne creatures, and it probably developed its gliding techniques to swoop down on its prey of insects.

# THE PTEROSAURS

The sinister-looking *pterosaurs* evolved into a great many different forms during the many millions of years when they swooped through the skies.

All had a lightweight skeleton of thin bones, and membranes of skin stretching from the ankles of their back legs to long fingers on the hands of the front legs. But their wingspan varied enormously. Some were no bigger than sparrows, whilst others had vast wings spanning a distance of 10 metres or more.

Most could not flap their wings, and simply glided on warm air currents from their cliff-top roosts. Others though, with strong breast muscles and shorter, broader wings, may have been able to flap, and so to fly in the true sense.

*Dimorphodon*, shown here, had a big skull and many sharp teeth.

## THE FURRY FOSSIL

In 1971, when the fossil remains of a *pterosaur* called *Sordes Pilosus* were found, they caused a sensation in the scientific world, for this creature was covered in thick fur. More research has yet to be done, but it could be that *pterosaurs* were not reptiles, after all, but warm-blooded, furry creatures.

# Questions and Answers

Here are the answers to some of the questions people most often ask about dinosaurs.

## WERE ALL DINOSAURS VICIOUS?

Not by any means. It is surprising how this idea persists even today, when a great deal of information is available about dinosaurs.

Through their evolution, there were many types of dinosaur which were exclusively plant-eaters. They would never have attacked another creature for food, and despite their often massive size they were often barely able to defend themselves against their cousins, the flesh-eaters.

Even the massive *Apatosaurus* (or *Brontosaurus* as it is more commonly known), for instance, was no match for the brutal killer of its time, *Allosaurus*.

## HOW DO SCIENTISTS FIND OUT ABOUT DINOSAURS?

Through the study of fossils. In the relatively short time in which scientists have been studying dinosaurs (only about 150 years), a tremendous amount of information has been yielded by fossil finds of one sort or another.

Sometimes the find will be a single bone, or even just a footprint preserved in hardened mud. On other, more rare occasions, a whole animal may be found, and such details as the skin or scales may have been preserved.

By painstaking work a group of bones found separately can sometimes be pieced together to make a whole skeleton.

## WHAT WAS THE MOST EXCITING FOSSIL FIND EVER?

All fossil finds are exciting, and scientists researching one particular area of the subject might well be overjoyed to find a single bone, perhaps, if it yielded some important clue in their work.

To the ordinary person interested in dinosaurs, however, a chance find by a group of Belgian coalminers in 1878 must surely rank as the most dramatic discovery of all time . . .

As they dug for coal near the village of Bernissart, the miners suddenly found that their picks were hacking into fossil bones. They had unearthed the site of a great catastrophe which had befallen an entire herd of *Iguanodon*, millions of years before. No less than 31 of them had somehow fallen into a ravine, and all had perished there.

## DID ALL DINOSAURS LIVE AT THE SAME TIME?

No. Over the Triassic, Jurassic and Cretaceous periods many different types evolved and died out. And of course there was some overlap between the periods. Not all Triassic dinosaurs, for instance, immediately died out when the Jurassic period began. They may themselves have continued to be successful, or their descendants may have gone on to evolve into more successful types.

## IS THERE ANYTHING LEFT TO FIND OUT ABOUT DINOSAURS?

Yes, a great deal!

No one can say exactly how many gaps there are in our knowledge of dinosaurs, nor whether the gaps will ever be filled. There may be entire groups of dinosaurs whose existence is not even suspected today. It's rather like a massive jigsaw puzzle, for which we don't yet have all the pieces.

After all, the history of the dinosaurs does span 140 million years!

# Jurassic Giants
# The Plant Eaters

The largest dinosaurs of the Jurassic period were true giants, with a terrifying appearance. And yet in reality they were slow-moving, peaceful creatures, who fed only on vegetation. In fact, as the saying goes, they wouldn't have hurt a fly!

## DIPLODOCUS

*Diplodocus* was an incredibly long animal. It spanned an astonishing 28 metres from its small head to the end of its whip-like tail.

On land it walked slowly on its four massive legs, but was more agile in its favourite habitat of swamps and muddy rivers, where it spent most of its time wading, and feeding on soft green vegetation. Its ten tonne weight was undoubtedly more comfortable when supported by the water.

*Diplodocus* had a very small head, and its brain was tiny too, being less than the size of a cat's or a dog's. Consequently, *Diplodocus* was rather dim-witted, and all too easy a prey for the vicious flesh-eaters of the time.

# APATOSAURUS
## or BRONTOSAURUS

*Apatosaurus,* as *Brontosaurus* is now more correctly known, was slightly shorter than *Diplodocus,* but even heavier, weighing in at anything up to 30 tonnes.

It too spent much of its time in swamps, walking mostly on its front legs, with its back legs kicking out behind, and the tail acting as a balance. It had nostrils at the top of its head so that it could breathe when almost completely submerged.

Fossilised footprints have shown *Apatosaurus* often walked in groups, and the young animals would be shepherded into the middle of the group for protection.

The name *Brontosaurus* means 'thunder lizard', and the animal was originally so-named because it was thought that its massive feet would have made a sound like thunder when it walked.

# BRACHIOSAURUS

The massive *Brachiosaurus* was another swamp wader, again equipped with nostrils placed high up on the head, so that the creature could breathe when its huge body was deep in the water.

*Brachiosaurus* was the largest land-going animal ever known, and its immense size required truly vast amounts of food to sustain it. When you consider that it ate only soft vegetation, you can get some idea of what a tremendous task this must have been. *Brachiosaurus* probably spent almost every waking hour feeding.

A full-grown man would not have reached to the joint in *Brachiosaurus'* leg, and at its full height it was taller than a three-storey house.

To get some idea of the great weights of these huge plant-eaters, it is useful to compare them with elephants. *Diplodocus* weighed about the same as two elephants; *Apatosaurus* weighed almost as much as six. As for *Brachiosaurus,* this massive creature weighed about 80 tonnes, which is comparable to the weight of 16 elephants.

The plant-eaters' peg-like teeth were poor at grinding leaves. The leaves had to be broken down to digestible pulp later, in the animal's enormous stomach.

# . . .and the Flesh Eaters

Massive though the Jurassic plant-eaters were, they were still no match for the vicious and powerful flesh-eaters of the time. A huge, slow-witted *Diplodocus,* for instance, which dared to venture out of the swamp for a while, would be an easy prey for the waiting *Allosaurus* . . .

## ALLOSAURUS

*Allosaurus* was probably the most brutal killer of all during the Jurassic period. It had enormous jaws, and ripped at its prey with sharp, 15cm teeth, possibly grunting with satisfaction during the kill.

Walking on hind legs, and making 2-metre strides, *Allosaurus* moved swiftly, swivelling its huge head from side to side and keeping a watch all around with its big beady eyes.

Though smaller than its victims, being about 12 metres long and weighing just 2 tonnes, *Allosaurus'* hunting skills, together with its lethal claws and teeth, were no match for its prey, and the plant-eaters were only safe from attack when submerged in the water.

# ORNITHOLESTES

When *Allosaurus* or one of the other flesh-eaters had made a kill, they would gorge themselves on the flesh for a while, and then move away to rest, just as many hunting animals do today. This would be the signal for *Ornitholestes* to move in.

This small dinosaur, only 2 metres long, was a scavenger, benefitting from the kills of the larger animals. Just like hyenas today, *Ornitholestes* provided a useful cleaning-up service in the Jurassic period, ensuring that the environment did not become contaminated with too many rotting dinosaur carcasses.

*Ornitholestes* was lightly built, with long, thin legs and a long, stiff tail. As well as scavenging it also caught some prey of its own, in the form of small reptiles, and the young of other dinosaurs. Its name actually means 'bird stealer', and it may indeed have caught some of the early *Archaeopteryx*.

# ARCHAEOPTERYX -
## the first bird

When the fossil remains of a creature called *Archaeopteryx* were found in Bavaria in 1861, it was a major breakthrough in the study of dinosaurs. For *Archaeopteryx* was the world's first bird.

The actual skeleton of *Archaeopteryx* was not much different from many small dinosaurs of the Jurassic period, such as *Compsognathus*, but one thing marked it out as being very different indeed.

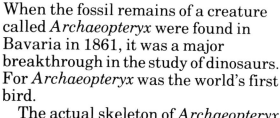

*Archaeopteryx* had feathers.

The feathers probably evolved from scales, gradually developing into wings, and there are two possible explanations as to why *Archaeopteryx* should have developed in this way.

It may originally have been a ground-dwelling creature, running and leaping after its prey, and the wings may have developed first of all to help it make swooping movements. Or it may have lived in the trees, and begun using its wings to parachute down, before they eventually became adapted to give lift and flapping flight.

Certainly the first *Archaeopteryx* types were not very strong fliers, and although they did have the air cavities in their bones which help modern day birds to fly, their breast muscles were not strong enough at first for much flapping of their wings.

*Archaeopteryx* had claws to help them in gripping and perching, both on their back legs and on front 'hands', but in one way they were different from birds as we know them today. They had numerous sharp teeth, with which they chewed their prey of insects and small lizards.

# ARCHAEOPTERYX v PTEROSAURS

*Archaeopteryx* lived at the same time as the *pterosaurs,* and it was *Archaeopteryx* which eventually became the more successful animal. This was for two main reasons.

Firstly, *Archaeopteryx* could live in dense woodland, swooping down amongst the trees for prey, where the *pterosaurs* dared not go. The *pterosaurs'* skin membranes were delicate, and if torn would not grow anew, but *Archaeopteryx's* feathers would part to avoid an obstacle, and even if they were damaged would grow again.

Also, *Archaeopteryx* was agile on the ground, once its wings were folded, whereas the *pterosaurs* were clumsy when grounded.

## WHAT DID ARCHAEOPTERYX LOOK LIKE?

Scientists have built up a clear picture of what *Archaeopteryx* must have looked like, but there is one thing which nobody can be certain about, and that is the colour of its plumage. Different types may have had different coloured plumage, and the males may have been more brightly coloured than the females, as with many modern day birds.

*Archaeopteryx* was about 60 cm long, and it used the sharp claws on its front 'hands' to catch prey, and also to cling to trees with its wings spread.

### 150 MILLION YEARS LATER . . .

Modern day birds have exactly the same number of feathers on their wings as *Archaeopteryx* had, and they are arranged in exactly the same way.

# Reptiles of the Jurassic seas

Three main groups of reptiles swam in the waters of the Jurassic seas: the ichthyosaurs, the plesiosaurs and the pliosaurs.

## PLESIOSAURS

Plesiosaurs were fish eaters, with long flexible necks and small heads.
Their four paddles acted as oars, and they could move backwards as well as forwards, and make rapid turns in the water.

Their paddles were not adapted for diving, however, and they probably spent most of their time paddling at the surface, and keeping their heads out of the water. Then when they spotted a fish, the long neck would stab the head down into the water to make the catch.

## WHAT A FIND!

Most of the knowledge which we have today about dinosaurs has come from studying fossilised evidence of their life on earth.
But it isn't always the experts who discover the fossils. The first skeletons of an *ichthyosaur* and a *plesiosaur* were found early in the nineteenth century, in Dorset, England by a girl of twelve.

## DID THEY REALLY DIE OUT?

Some people believe that modern day 'lake monsters', of which the most famous is Scotland's Nessie of Loch Ness, may in fact be huge creatures left over from the age of the dinosaurs. If that's true, Nessie's long neck would indicate that she is most likely to be some type of *plesiosaur*.

# ICHTHYOSAURS

Ichthyosaurs were up to 12 metres long, with large tail fins, triangular back fins and fin-like paddles. They were strong swimmers, hunting for fish which they snapped up with the numerous sharp teeth in their long, narrow snouts.

Fossilised droppings have shown much evidence that they ate a fast-swimming fish called Pholidophorus, which swam near the surface of the sea.

Interestingly, the fossilised stomach contents of other ichthyosaurs suggest that some of the later ones may have changed their diet. One young ichthyosaur, less than 2 metres long, was found to have eaten nearly 1600 cephalopods, which were early relatives of the octopus. The ichthyosaur's stomach contained nearly 500,000 of the small, indigestible, black hooks which grew on the cephalopods' tentacles.

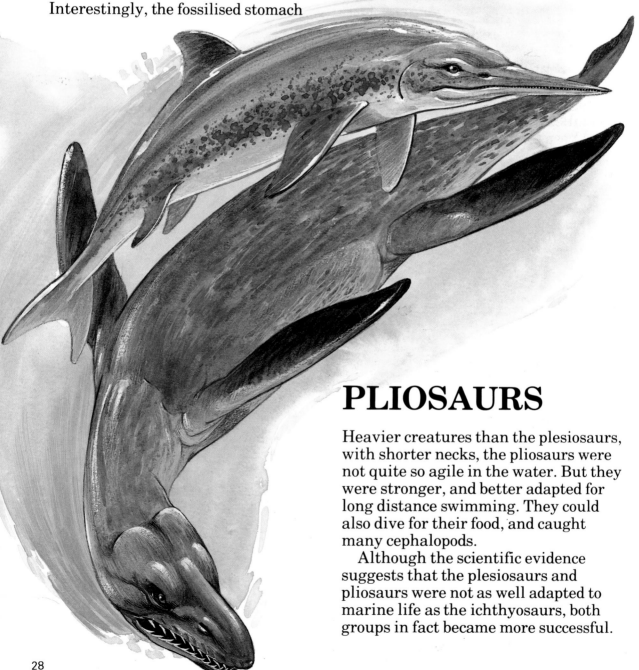

# PLIOSAURS

Heavier creatures than the plesiosaurs, with shorter necks, the pliosaurs were not quite so agile in the water. But they were stronger, and better adapted for long distance swimming. They could also dive for their food, and caught many cephalopods.

Although the scientific evidence suggests that the plesiosaurs and pliosaurs were not as well adapted to marine life as the ichthyosaurs, both groups in fact became more successful.

# Questions and Answers

## WERE ALL DINOSAURS HUGE?

No. Dinosaurs varied greatly in size.
We tend to read more about the
absolutely massive ones, because they
seem so strange and exciting, but in fact
many dinosaurs were no bigger than
the common animals of today.
The smallest dinosaur ever is believed
to have been *Compsognathus,* of the
Jurassic period. At 30 cm long when
fully grown, this creature was no bigger
than a farmyard hen. It probably lived
on small mammals, lizards and insects.

## WERE ANY OTHER ANIMALS ALIVE AT THE SAME TIME AS THE DINOSAURS?

Yes, there was a tremendous variety of
animal life, just as there is today.
Before *Archaeopteryx* there were no
birds as such, and snakes did not appear
until the *Cretaceous* period, but there
were all manner of other creatures,
including, no doubt, some which are
now extinct, and of which we have found
no evidence. The first true mammals
were probably shrew-like creatures,
feeding on insects.

# COULD DINOSAURS HAVE BEEN WARM-BLOODED?

Dinosaurs certainly did have a better blood supply than the cold-blooded reptiles we know today, but they are still classed as reptiles by most scientists. There are some experts, however, who believe that the dinosaurs may indeed have been warm-blooded, as mammals are. This is currently the subject of much discussion and debate.

# WHAT WAS SUPERSAURUS?

*Brachiosaurus* is generally described as being the biggest land-going animal that ever lived, with its relative, *Diplodocus*, taking the prize for the greatest length. But a fossil find in Colorado in 1972 has set the experts wondering if a larger creature still once roamed the earth. The bones suggest that a creature once existed which weighed no less than two and a half times as much as *Brachiosaurus*. Little wonder that this true giant was soon dubbed *Supersaurus!*

# King of the Tyrant Lizards

The largest flesh-eater of all time . . . a massive, walking predatory machine . . . *Tyrannosaurus Rex* well deserves its name, which literally means 'king of the tyrant lizards'.

This terrifying animal weighed 7 tonnes. It was 15 metres long, and up to 6 metres tall.

Just imagine, if one of these fearsome creatures walked down a street of ordinary two-storey houses today, it could quite comfortably peer into all the upstairs windows.

*Tyrannosaurus Rex* always walked upright on its two back legs, and its footprints measured 75 cm in each direction. It took relatively short strides of around 1 metre, and must have had a waddling sort of gait.

It probably wasn't very agile, and

relied on its great strength when hunting its prey of defenceless plant-eaters. One good kill would have lasted it for weeks, perhaps even months, and for days after feasting on a kill it would lie about drowsily, thoroughly bloated.

The three claws on its hind toes were its most powerful weapon — the teeth would mostly be used for tearing the flesh after a kill had been made — and they were as deadly and sharp as meat knives.

In contrast to the massive back legs, the front ones were short, and too weak to use as weapons. They were mostly

used to activate the massive shoulder muscles which raised the animal after it had been lying down.

A very successful dinosaur, *Tyrannosaurus Rex* survived right until the end of the Cretaceous period.

A *Tyrannosaurus Rex* was one of the first complete fossil skeletons to be found by Othniel Marsh and Edward Drinker Cope in Colorado, in the nineteenth century. Those first skeletons convinced a dis believing public that these giant creatures really had existed.

The massive, mighty jaws carried 50 fang-like teeth as long as a man's hand. When any of the teeth broke, others would soon grow to replace them.

Each beady eye was set in a socket as large as a child's head. It was 'curtains' for any poor plant-eater one of *those* eyes settled on!

# The Walking Tanks

It was always very important for the plant-eating dinosaurs to protect themselves from attack by the fierce flesh-eaters, and the *ankylosaurs* evolved a particularly effective means of defence.

They grew a thick, bony covering of protective 'armour', which was strong enough to break the teeth of any enemy which chanced to take a bite. Walking as they did, close to the ground on all fours, the soft, vulnerable belly was shielded by the impenetrable top covering.

Several slightly different types of armour evolved.

## POLACANTHUS

One of the earliest *ankylosaurs* was *Polacanthus*. It had rows of tall, bony spikes sticking upwards from its head and part of its back. The hip area was protected by a bony shield, and a crest of bony triangles ensured that the tail was safe from attack, too.

# PALAEOSCINCUS

*Palaeoscincus* was possibly the best-protected *ankylosaur* of all. Most enemies would probably try to aim a blow beneath the armour, to penetrate the soft underbelly, but this would have been impossible with *Palaeoscincus*. Low down at the sides, a row of sharp spikes effectively prevented any enemy approach.

# EUOPLOCEPHALUS

This creature used to be called *Ankylosaurus*, and from it the *ankylosaurs* took their name. Sharp-edged plates covered the animal's back, from its head to its tail. The long tail ended in a kind of bony club, and it may well have lashed out with this if under attack. *Euoplocephalus* was about the size of an estate car.

The *ankylosaurs* were related to an earlier animal, *Stegosaurus,* from the Jurassic period. This 9 metre long creature was protected by bony plates, up to 1 metre long, which grew in pairs along its back. *Stegosaurus* looked frightening, but in fact was a slow-moving, dim-witted animal, with a brain no bigger than a walnut!

Another distinctive *hadrosaur* was *Corythosaurus,* which lived in swampy areas.

# The Duck-Bills . . .

The *hadrosaurs*, or duck-billed dinosaurs, were very odd-looking creatures.

They walked on three-toed hind legs, using their long, flattened tails for balance as they browsed on the leaves of trees. They had literally hundreds of teeth in their long, wide jaws.

But the oddest thing about them were the bony crests which sprouted from the backs of their skulls.

One of the most distinctive of these crests was that of *Parasaurolophus*, shown here, which curved backwards from the top of the head.

*Hadrosaurs* were a very successful group of dinosaurs, and many different types evolved. Each had its own particular type of crest, which was probably the way in which each type recognised others of its own kind.

# ... And the Bone-Heads

Bone-headed dinosaurs got their name because of their incredibly thick, bony skulls.

They varied in size, and one of the first was *Yaverlandia*, which was only about the size of a turkey. Later they grew bigger, and their skulls grew thicker.

*Stegoceras*, for instance, was about the size of a man, though its brain was smaller than a tennis ball. Protecting this small brain, however, was a skull some five times as thick as a man's.

And in *Pachycephalosaurus*, shown here 'in action', the skull was an amazing 20 times thicker than a man's.

Experts are not entirely sure of the purpose of this exceptional protective casing, but it may be that it developed from fights between males over leadership of herds.

They probably banged their heads together during these important 'duels', although neither animal would be fighting to kill. Protected as they were by their skulls the jarring shock would be felt down their backs, and probably eventually one or other of the adversaries would concede defeat.

# The Horned and Frilled Dinosaurs

These startling-looking dinosaurs were some of the few which would have dared to mount an attack on one of the fierce flesh-eaters. Some experts think that even a full grown *Tyrannosaurus Rex* might have turned tail and run from a charging *Triceratops*.

Properly called *ceratopsians*, these animals grew larger as the different types evolved, and their horns grew stronger.

The purpose of the alarming-looking bony 'frill', however, was probably not only protective, as was at first supposed. It would also have increased the strength of the jaw muscles. With their bite thus improved, the *ceratopsians* could eat tougher plant foods, such as palm fronds.

# TRICERATOPS

The largest of all the horned and frilled dinosaurs, *Triceratops* could weigh up to 8 tonnes. It had three horns, and long rows of teeth which it used for ripping its food from the trees. It could be anything up to 11 metres in length, and was the most formidable of all the *ceratopsians*.

# PENTACERATOPS

*Pentaceratops* was one of the 'long-frilled' *ceratopsians*.

All the *ceratopsians* were descended from a dinosaur called *Psittacosaurus*, whose name means 'parrot lizard'. This was an important creature in the history of the dinosaurs, because it was the first one with the apparent ability to walk well on either two or four legs. It was only 2 metres long, much smaller than *Triceratops*, which was to come later, and it had a strange appearance because of its hooked 'beak'.

# STYRACOSAURUS

The frill of *Styracosaurus* ended in an array of spikes.

# The Coelurosaurs

The bird-like *coelurosaurs* looked like nothing so much as plucked ostriches! They had long legs and necks, and a long tail, and their arms ended in sharp-clawed hands.

They probably lived to a large extent on the eggs of other dinosaurs, and they would scoop away the sand from a nest of eggs with their hands. Then they would smash open the shells to get at the food inside.

Other items in their diet might have been small lizards, fruit, or perhaps the teeming occupants of an ants' nest.

**ORNITHOMIMUS**

Being smaller than the fierce flesh-eaters, *the coelurosaurs* used speed as their best defence when under attack. It is thought that they could run as fast as 80 m.p.h. That would be an incredible speed for a reptile, so it is possible that they were not true dinosaurs, after all.

**STRUTHIOMIMUS**

# Questions and Answers

## WHO WERE MARSH AND COPE?

Othniel Marsh was an American palaeontologist, and Edward Drinker Cope was a naturalist. Both were working in the second half of the nineteenth century, and both were passionately interested in researching dinosaur bones and identifying new species. They became great rivals. Each of them regularly sent out teams of hired fossil hunters, and all sorts of spying and trickery went on as the rival teams vied for the best finds. On one occasion, two teams actually came to blows! Both Marsh and Cope contributed a tremendous amount of information to dinosaur research.

## DID DINOSAURS FIGHT?

Exciting films and dramatic comic book stories often show the vicious flesh-eating dinosaurs fighting each other, and it is reasonable to assume that fights must have occurred, when food was scarce, for instance, or perhaps over territorial disputes. Interestingly though, there is no fossil evidence of two flesh-eaters fighting. There is an

*Apatosaur* skeleton in The American Museum whose tail bears *Allosaurus* teeth marks, and there was a very dramatic fossil find in Mongolia in 1971, where two dinosaurs were locked in combat. But both these finds were of a flesh-eater attacking a plant-eater.

# WHY DID DINOSAURS BECOME EXTINCT?

This is a great mystery. Fossil evidence proves conclusively that round about 64 million years ago the dinosaurs became completely extinct — and it seems to have happened in a very short period of time. This is particularly odd because they are known to have been highly adaptable creatures, evolving very successfully to suit their environment. There are numerous theories as to their extinction. Many concern climatic change, and one theory holds that there may have been some sudden, cataclysmic weather condition which affected the whole world. Another, more complex idea suggests that for various reasons the balance of male and female animals may have become unstable, and that successful breeding may have become impossible.

## ISN'T IT POSSIBLE THAT EVEN ONE SPECIES MAY HAVE SURVIVED?

Well yes, it is *just* possible! Some people believe that 'lake monsters' — for instance our own Loch Ness monster — may be living examples of *plesiosaurs* which are still existing in deep, dark waters. You don't believe it? Then think about the *Coelacanth*. This fish was thought to have been extinct for 70 million years — until one was caught by a trawler in 1938. Since then, many more have been found.

# DINOSAUR DICTIONARY

An alphabetical glossary of some familiar and unfamiliar dinosaur words.

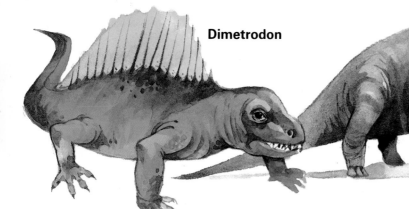

Dimetrodon

Brachiosaurus

Archelon

crocodile

| | |
|---|---|
| **Archelon** | This huge marine turtle flourished during the Cretaceous period. It was 4 metres long, and its name means 'ruler turtle'. |
| **Bernissart** | In 1878 coal miners in this Belgian village made an amazing find of *Iguanodon* bones. |
| **Brachiosaurus** | The largest land-going animal ever. |
| **cockroach** | Cockroaches are very ancient insects. They are known to have lived over 300 million years ago. |
| **coprolite** | A fossilised animal dropping. |
| **crocodile** | The only living reptile directly related to dinosaurs, the crocodile has remained almost unchanged for 200 million years. |
| **Dimetrodon** | One of the paramammals, *Dimetrodon* had a large, sail-like fin on its back. |
| **dinosaur** | Literally means 'terrible lizard'. |
| **egg** | Dinosaurs were egg-laying reptiles. |
| **Elasmosaurus** | A serpent-like marine reptile with a very long neck. Many fossils have been found in clay near Peterborough, England. |
| **footprint** | Fossilised footprints in sand and mud are fascinating finds for scientists. |
| **geology** | Science which investigates the history and structure of the earth. |
| **Gondwanaland** | Name of the southern land mass when the earth had only one continent, Pangea. |

| | |
|---|---|
| **Gorgosaurus** | A huge flesh-eating dinosaur. It had an enormous mouth and many small, lethal teeth. |
| **Graculavus** | A fishing cormorant of the late Cretaceous period. |
| **hadrosaurs** | 'Duck-billed' dinosaurs of the Cretaceous period. |
| **Hesperornis** | A flightless, swimming bird of the Cretaceous period. It was a toothed fish-eater. |
| **Hypsilophodon** | One of the most successful dinosaurs, probably because of its speed when running. It was only 60 cm high. |
| **Iguanodon** | This was the first dinosaur to be completely identified from fossil remains. A plant-eater, it protected itself with its sharp pointed thumbs, which could rip out the eye of an attacker. All the *hadrosaurs* were related to *Iguanodon*. |
| **jellyfish** | Jellyfish lived in the lagoons of the Jurassic period, and many well-preserved specimens from that time have been found. |
| **Kentrosaurus** | An African relative of *Stegosaurus,* with long spikes in pairs over its back and down its tail. |
| **lagoon** | An enclosed area of sea. |
| **Lambeosaurus** | A duck-billed dinosaur with a large, hatchet-shaped crest projecting from behind its head. |
| **Laurasia** | The northern land mass in the continent of Pangea. |

**Iguanodon**

**Gorgosaurus**

**Hadrosaur**

**Hypsilophodon**

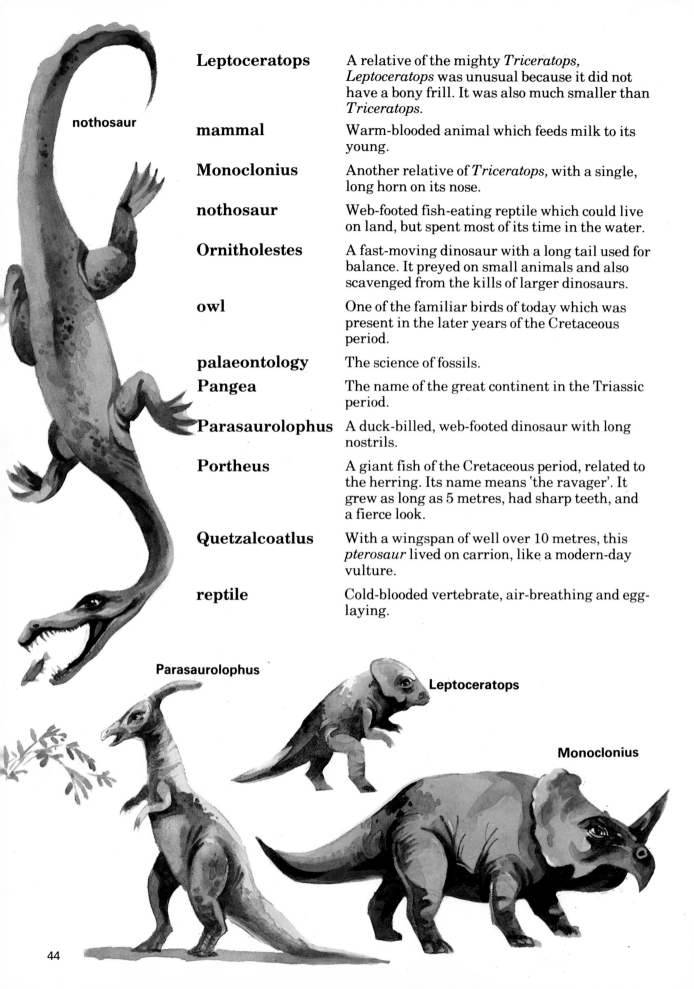

**nothosaur**

|  |  |
|---|---|
| **Leptoceratops** | A relative of the mighty *Triceratops*, *Leptoceratops* was unusual because it did not have a bony frill. It was also much smaller than *Triceratops*. |
| **mammal** | Warm-blooded animal which feeds milk to its young. |
| **Monoclonius** | Another relative of *Triceratops*, with a single, long horn on its nose. |
| **nothosaur** | Web-footed fish-eating reptile which could live on land, but spent most of its time in the water. |
| **Ornitholestes** | A fast-moving dinosaur with a long tail used for balance. It preyed on small animals and also scavenged from the kills of larger dinosaurs. |
| **owl** | One of the familiar birds of today which was present in the later years of the Cretaceous period. |
| **palaeontology** | The science of fossils. |
| **Pangea** | The name of the great continent in the Triassic period. |
| **Parasaurolophus** | A duck-billed, web-footed dinosaur with long nostrils. |
| **Portheus** | A giant fish of the Cretaceous period, related to the herring. Its name means 'the ravager'. It grew as long as 5 metres, had sharp teeth, and a fierce look. |
| **Quetzalcoatlus** | With a wingspan of well over 10 metres, this *pterosaur* lived on carrion, like a modern-day vulture. |
| **reptile** | Cold-blooded vertebrate, air-breathing and egg-laying. |

**Parasaurolophus**

**Leptoceratops**

**Monoclonius**

**Rhamphorhynchus**

**Styracosaurus**

| | |
|---|---|
| **Rhamphorhynchus** | A *pterosaur* of the Jurassic period, its name literally means 'prow beak', because its beak was shaped like the prow of a boat. |
| **scavenger** | Animal which feeds on the remains of kills made by other animals. |
| **Strutheomimus** | An ostrich-like Cretaceous dinosaur, less than 2 metres high. It was an egg-stealer. |
| **Styracosaurus** | A 5 metre long *ceratopsian* with many horns around its neck. Its name means 'spiked lizard'. |
| **Tethys** | The name of the great ocean to the east of the continent of Pangea in the Triassic period. |
| **Trachodon** | A duck-billed dinosaur. It had four rows of chewing teeth, which in all numbered 2,000! |
| **Usbekistan** | Many fossil remains have been found in Cretaceous rocks in Usbekistan. |
| **Velociraptor** | A flesh-eater of the Cretaceous period. |
| **vertebrate** | An animal with a backbone. |
| **Wurttemberg** | Area of Germany where many important *ichthyosaur* skeletons were found. These were remarkably well-preserved and yielded much information. |
| **e-X-tinct** | Dinosaurs are e-X-tinct! Or are they? |
| **Yaverlandia** | Probably the first of the bone-headed dinosaurs, *Yaverlandia* was about the size of a turkey, with a long tail. |
| **Youngina** | A small, insect-eating reptile, one of a group which preceded the dinosaurs. They were land-dwellers, and walked with a clumsy gait, holding their legs out sideways. |
| **zoo** | A dinosaur is a creature you *won't* find in any zoo! |

**Strutheomimus**

**plesiosaur**